Stepping Out

On the Pathway to Your Dreams

Compiled by
PAM FARREL

Paintings by
SANDY LYNAM CLOUGH

HARVEST HOUSE PUBLISHERS
Eugene, Oregon

Stepping Out
Copyright © 1999 Harvest House Publishers
Eugene, Oregon 97402

Library of Congress Cataloging-in-Publication Data
  Stepping out / compiled by Pam Farrel ; paintings by Sandy Lynam Clough.
       p.   cm.
    ISBN 1-56507-902-7
    1. Women—Quotations.   I. Farrel, Pam. 1959-
    PN6081.5.S74   1999
    082'.082—dc21
                                                    98-42881
                                                      CIP

Stepping Out

If the shoe fits…wear it!

If the dream fits…step into it!

We all have hopes and dreams that we long to see fulfilled. On the pages of this book are quotes from women who have stepped out into their dreams. May their words encourage you as you step out and live your own dreams. May their words inspire you to keep putting one foot in front of the other in your journey toward personal success. May their words also congratulate you as you step across the finish line. And all along your pathway, may you find joy in stepping out!

One Step at a Time

As a gymnast growing up, my favorite event was the balance beam—not because I was a flawless champion but because of the thrill. There was a rush, knowing that each step mattered as I danced, spun, and sometimes teetered at the edge, high above the ground. The thrill was in the risk.

Life is like that. The jazz of life is not found in the comfort zone but in the steps of courage you take to become all you were designed to be. Mountains that seem impossible can be scaled one step at a time. Fear and worry are counterproductive. Don't get distracted by what can't be done. Focus on what **can** be done today, even if it is just one small step!

Small steps taken consistently add up in a big way over time.

DANNA DEMETRE

Sandy Lynam Clough

Do the next thing.

ELISABETH ELLIOT

You better live your best and act your best and
think your best today; for today is the sure
preparation for tomorrow and all the other
tomorrows that follow.

LIFE'S USES

*There is
no magic in
small plans.*

HENRIETTA MEARS

*It is important to know I have
a source of strength beyond my own.*

ELIZABETH DOLE

First woman president of the Red Cross since its founder, Clara Barton

*It is only the first step
that is difficult.*

MARIE DE VICHY-CHAMROND

Reach high,

for stars lie hidden in your soul.

Dream deep,

for every dream precedes the goal.

PAMELA VAULL STARR

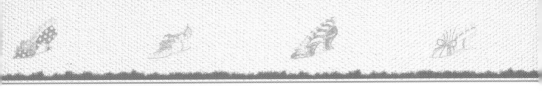

Optimism is the faith that leads to
achievement.
Nothing can be done without hope.

*Ask, and it will be given to you;
seek, and you will find; knock,
and it will be opened to you.*

*Now faith is being sure of what we hope for
and certain of what we do not see.*

Faith isn't the ability to believe long and far into the misty future.
It's simply taking God at His word and taking the next step.

JONI EARECKSON TADA

*Where reasons are given,
we don't need faith. Where only
darkness surrounds us, we have no
means for seeing except by faith.*

ELISABETH ELLIOT

14

Far away, there in the
sunshine, are my highest
aspirations.
I may not reach them but I
can look up and see their
beauty, believe in them,
and try to follow where
they lead.

LOUISA MAY ALCOTT

I discovered I always have choices, and sometimes it's only a choice of attitude.

JUDITH M. KNOWLTON

Courage is fear that has said its prayers.

DOROTHY BERNARD

The secret of getting ahead is getting started.

SALLY BERGER

It is for us to pray not for tasks equal to our powers,

but for powers equal to our tasks,

to go forward with a great desire forever

beating at the door of our hearts

as we travel towards our distant goal.

HELEN KELLER

Instead of worry,

try investigation and innovation.

Instead of complaining, try creativity.

PAM FARREL

When you do nothing, you feel overwhelmed and powerless. But when you get involved, you feel the sense of hope and accomplishment that comes from knowing you are working to make things better.

PAULINE R. KEZER

If you know what you are
doing, if you
believe in what you're doing,
you can make it....

REVA YARES

21

Step Up!

As a child, I loved to run in the sprinkler and then onto the sidewalk, leaving my footprints on the hot cement. I would soon be disappointed, though, as the warmth of the sun evaporated my temporary prints.

Footprints we leave on the hearts of those around us, though, are forever. When we choose to step out, we make a difference. A friend has this story framed on her wall: An older woman is walking along the beach, throwing starfish back into the sea so they can live. A younger woman, watching the scene and seeing the waves endlessly toss starfish back onto the beach, asks the older woman, "Why are you doing this? There are so many starfish, and you are just one person. What difference is it making?" The older woman picks up a starfish, tosses it into the sea, and says, "It made a difference to that one."

What you are is God's gift to you. What you can become is your gift to Him.

HENRIETTA MEARS

Be you. Be the very best you. It is a gift that only you can give yourself.

PAM FARREL

No pessimist ever discovered the secrets of the stars, or sailed to an uncharted land, or opened a new heaven to the human spirit.

HELEN KELLER

Worry does not

empty tomorrow of

its sorrow;

it empties today

of its strength.

CORRIE TEN BOOM

I am only one; but still I am one.
I cannot do everything, but still I can
do something; I will not refuse to do the
something I can do.

HELEN KELLER

As we have opportunity,
let us do good to all people.

THE BOOK OF GALATIANS

*The timeless wisdom that is
passed from woman to woman is
one of life's greatest gifts.*

ANONYMOUS

The trouble with

the rat race is that

even if you win,

you're still a rat.

LILY TOMLIN

*God has not called me
to be successful;
he has called me
to be faithful.*

MOTHER TERESA

To gain that which is worth having,
it may be necessary to lose everything else.

BERNADETTE DEVLIN

Life is under no obligation to give us what we expect.

MARGARET MITCHELL

The choices I make about what I do with my time are my choices
(even when they don't appear to be).

ANNE WILSON SHAEF

It is never too late to be what you might have been.

GEORGE ELIOT

It's easier to act your way

into new ways of

feeling than to feel yourself

into new ways of acting.

SUSAN GLASER

You may have to fight a battle more than once to win it.

MARGARET THATCHER

Let nothing disturb you.
Let nothing frighten you.
Everything passes away except God.

SAINT THERESA

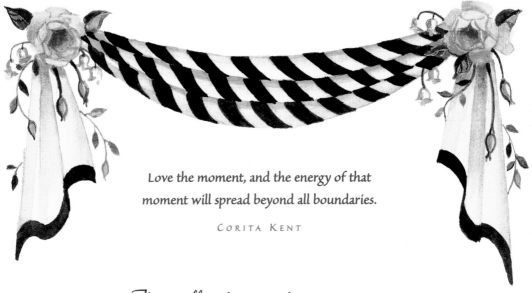

Love the moment, and the energy of that
moment will spread beyond all boundaries.

CORITA KENT

The excellent becomes the permanent.

JANE ADDAMS

Step Out!

Mother eagles are very strategic. For months they carefully pad their nest with bits of string, leaves, and debris to build a soft, cozy haven. But to get her babies to soar when the time comes, the mother eagle begins to take out the cushion, tossing the comfort over the cliffs until the nest is very rugged and uncomfortable. Then her young ones are pushed out of the nest and into the air to soar.

Being comfortable teaches us to be comfortable. Learning to fly always starts out feeling like a crisis!

People don't change until the pain of their life becomes greater than the pain of change.

A MARY KAY CORPORATION
TRAINING TAPE

A bird does not know it can fly

before it uses its wings.

We learn God's love in our hearts

as soon as we act upon it.

CORRIE TEN BOOM

My crown should erase the word *impossible.*

HEATHER WHITESTONE

FIRST DEAF MISS AMERICA

I don't wait for moods.

You accomplish nothing if you do that.

Your mind must know it has got to get

down to earth.

PEARL S. BUCK

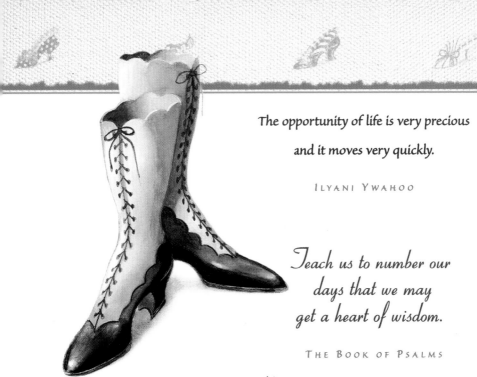

The opportunity of life is very precious
and it moves very quickly.

ILYANI YWAHOO

*Teach us to number our
days that we may
get a heart of wisdom.*

THE BOOK OF PSALMS

41

Run your race to win.

THE BOOK OF 1 CORINTHIANS

God created us with an
overwhelming desire to soar...
He designed us to be tremendously
productive and "to mount up with wings
like eagles," realistically dreaming of what
he can do with our potential.

CAROL KENT

When one door of happiness closes, another opens:
but often we look so long at the closed door that
we do not see the one which has been opened for us.

HELEN KELLER

44

Forgetting the past and looking forward to what lies ahead...

THE BOOK OF PHILIPPIANS

You gain strength, courage and confidence by every experience in
which you really stop to look fear in the face....
You must do the thing which you think you cannot.

ELEANOR ROOSEVELT

45

I pray hard, work hard,
and leave the rest to God.

FLORENCE GRIFFITH JOYNER

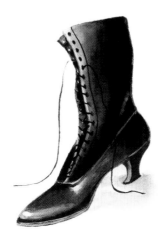

You must accept that you might fail; then, if you do your best and still don't win, at least you can be satisfied that you've tried. If you don't accept failure as a possibility, you don't set high goals, you don't branch out, you don't try—you don't take the risk.

ROSALYNN CARTER

In Step!

Dancing in step takes talent. Marching in step takes discipline. And getting people to work in step takes leadership!

Most of the time, each of us feels incredibly ordinary, but that shouldn't hold us back. One ordinary woman can make a difference. Our job is to get in step with the purpose for which we were created. The world is longing for women who will make a difference. Women make great leaders! Faith Whittlesey said it best: "Remember, Ginger Rogers did everything Fred Astaire did, but she did it backwards and in high heels."

You can't, God never said you could;
He can, God always said
He would.

JILL BRISCOE

When you cease to make
a contribution you begin to die.

ELEANOR ROOSEVELT

I am not afraid of storms, for I am learning how to sail my ship.

LOUISA MAY ALCOTT

Perseverance

makes

impossible

opportunities

possible.

PAM FARREL

51

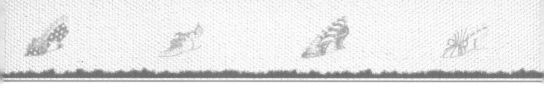

*It is not fair
to ask of others
what you are not willing
to do yourself.*

ELEANOR ROOSVELT

If you have made mistakes…there is always another chance for you….
You may have a fresh start any moment you choose, for this thing we
call "failure" is not the falling down, but the staying down.

MARY PICKFORD

She who hangs in
the longest—wins.

PAM FARREL

You can't change circumstances and you can't change other people, but God can change you.

EVELYN THIESSEN

*Winning the prize
wasn't half as exciting as
doing the work itself.*

MARIA GUEPPERT MAYER

Winner of the 1963 Nobel Prize in physics

Since future victory is sure, be strong and steady.

THE BOOK OF 1 CORINTHIANS

Creativity is inventing,

experimenting, growing,

taking risks, breaking rules,

making mistakes,

and having fun.

MARY LOU COOK

*Take your work seriously,
but never yourself.*

DAME MARGOT
FONTEYN

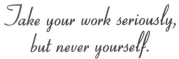

Give her of the fruit of her hands,
and let her own works praise her
in the gates.

THE BOOK OF PROVERBS

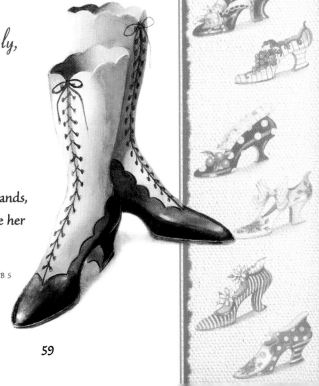

What you have become is the price you paid to get what you used to want.

MIGNON McLAUGHLIN

60

So many women just don't know
how great they really are.
They come to us all vogue outside
and vague on the inside.

MARY KAY ASH

Class is an aura of confidence that is

being sure without being cocky.

Class has nothing to do with money.

Class never runs scared.

It is self-discipline and self-knowledge.

It's the surefootedness

that comes with having proved you can meet life.

ANN LANDERS

Figure out what your most magnificent qualities are and make them indispensable to the people you work with. Notice that I didn't say "work for."

LINDA BLOODWORTH-THOMASON

Remember, no one can make you

feel inferior without your consent.

ELEANOR ROOSEVELT